egasystems **PEGAPCDC74V1**

Pega Certified Decisioning Consultant
Version: 1.0

QUESTION NO: 1 CORRECT TEXT

Results of two simulations can be compared using the ______________.

Answer:
Visual Business Director

Answer:
Interaction History report

Answer:
Proposition Distribution report

Answer:
Predictive Analytics Director

Answer:
A

Reference: https://pegasystems2.https.internapcdn.net/pegasystems2/marketing/C-762-StudentGuide.pdf (124)

QUESTION NO: 2

Which of the following is a dimension in Visual Business Director?

A.
Revenue

B.
Channel

C.
Volume

D.
Intent

Answer: B
Reference: https://community1.pega.com/community/pega-support/question/what-are-6-dimensions-visual-business-director

Which is a Key Performance Indicator?

A.

Action

B.

Outcome

C.

Volume

D.

Channel

Answer: A

Explanation:

QUESTION NO: 4

Visual Business Director can be used to ______________.

A.

inspect interactions of a single customer

B.

compare two datasets

C.

predict customer behavior

D.

import and inspect and external dataset

Answer: B

Explanation:

QUESTION NO: 5

Which metric is used in the Proposition Distribution report?

A.

cept rate

B.

Volume

C.

Target budget

D.

Total revenue

Answer: A

Explanation:

QUESTION NO: 6

To build a predictive model, use ____________.

A.

Pega Customer Service

B.

Pega Marketing

C.

Pega Decision Management

D.

Pega Platform

Answer: D

Reference: https://community.pega.com/sites/default/files/help_v73/dsm/da-portal/tasks/da-creating-predictive-model-tsk.htm

QUESTION NO: 7

Next-Best-Action maximizes the customer lifetime value by ____________.

A.

using consistency rules in the Next-Best-Action decision strategy

B.

building Next-Best-Action on top of each other across every interaction

C.

monitoring the customer interactions in all channels

D.

using arbitration metrics in the Next-Best-Action decision strategy

Answer: C

Explanation:

QUESTION NO: 8

The implementation of Next-Best-Action must involve _______________.

A.

building a product catalog

B.

defining business issue and group hierarchy

C.

inclusion of third party predictive models

D.

defining a prioritization formula based on marketing weight

Answer: B

Explanation:

QUESTION NO: 9

What is the key characteristic that Next-Best-Action must consider to satisfy customer needs?

A.

Service

B.

Consistency

C.

Mobility

Answer: B

Explanation:

QUESTION NO: 10

Which business issue is the least suitable for Next-Best-Action?

A.
Collections

B.
Retention

C.
Service

D.
Accounting

Answer: D

Explanation:

QUESTION NO: 11

Business rules that determine if a customer is eligible for a particular proposition are also known as
______________.

A.
Contact rules

B.
Hard rules

C.
Soft rules

D.
Marketing rules

Answer: A

Reference: https://pegasystems2.https.internapcdn.net/pegasystems2/marketing/C-762-

QUESTION NO: 12

One of the flow shapes which allows seamless integration of Pega Decision Management with Pega Business Process Management is ______________.

A.

Subprocess

B.

Strategy Flow

C.

Utility

D.

Decision

Answer: D

Reference: http://smartrules.nl/part-3-more-layers/

QUESTION NO: 13

To which types of decisions can Decision Management be applied?

A.

Determining the cause of a customer's problem

B.

Determining why response rates for a campaign in one region are below average

C.

Determining how to retain a customer and what budget we should spend

D.

Determining how to optimize the product portfolio to increase market share

Answer: B

Explanation:

Which decision component is used to arbitrate between propositions?

A.
Prioritize

B.
Adjudication

C.
Arbitration

D.
Decision Table

Answer: C
Explanation:

QUESTION NO: 15

In a prioritization expression, to balance the customer needs and business objectives you adjust
_______________.

A.
customer contact rules

B.
weights and levels

C.
product compatibility rules

D.
product eligibility rules

Answer: B
Reference: https://pegasystems2.https.internapcdn.net/pegasystems2/marketing/C-762-
StudentGuide.pdf

QUESTION NO: 16

The Next-Best-Action strategies must be _______________.

secured and modified only by IT

B.

simple and straight forward

C.

easy to be changed by the business

D.

complex and forensically calculated

Answer: B

Explanation:

QUESTION NO: 17

Which decision component is used to implement hard rules?

A.

Prioritize

B.

Adaptive Model

C.

Decision Table

D.

Eligibility

Answer: D

Reference: https://community1.pega.com/community/product-support/question/dsm-relevant-information-soft-rules-and-hard-rules

QUESTION NO: 18

The Predictive Model Markup Language (PMML) allows for predictive models to ___________ .

A.

be developed faster

be easily shared between applications

C.

use the same modelling process

D.

perform better

Answer: B

Reference: https://pegasystems2.https.internapcdn.net/pegasystems2/marketing/C-762-
StudentGuide.pdf

QUESTION NO: 19

When compared to a Predictive Model, an Adaptive Model is different as it ___________.

A.

can use strategy properties as predictors

B.

considers both symbolic and numeric predictors

C.

learns from both positive and negative outcomes

D.

uses predictor binning

Answer: C

Reference: https://pegasystems2.https.internapcdn.net/pegasystems2/marketing/C-762-
StudentGuide.pdf

QUESTION NO: 20

What is the difference between predictive and adaptive analytics?

A.

Predictive models can predict a continuous value.

B.

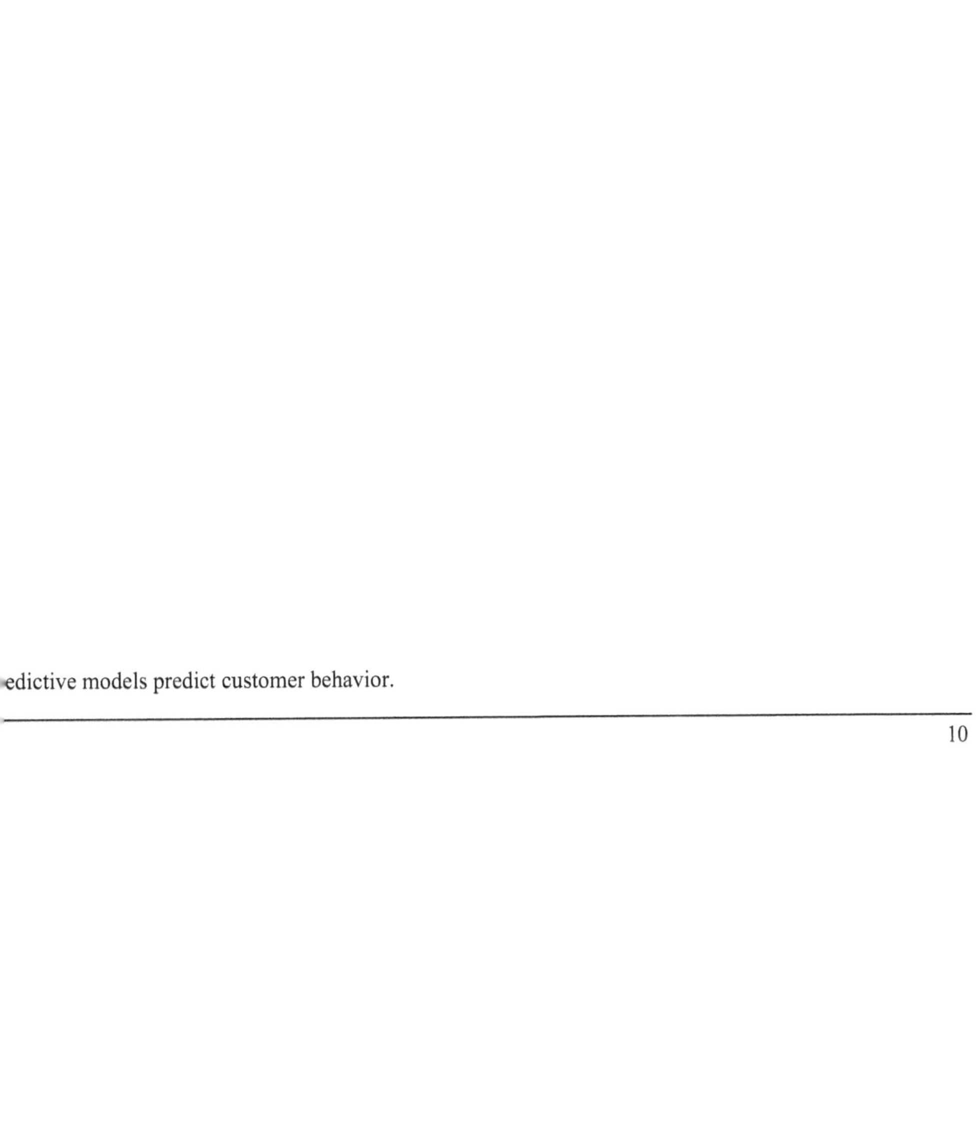

edictive models predict customer behavior.

C.

Adaptive models use the customer data as predictors.

D.

Predictive models have evidence.

Answer: C

Reference: https://pegasystems2.https.internapcdn.net/pegasystems2/marketing/C-762-StudentGuide.pdf

QUESTION NO: 21

The likelihood that a proposition will be accepted by the customer is stored in the strategy property called
________________.

A.

pyPropensity

B.

pyLikelihood

C.

pyProbability

D.

pyBehavior

Answer: A

Reference: https://pegasystems2.https.internapcdn.net/pegasystems2/marketing/C-762-StudentGuide.pdf

QUESTION NO: 22

Two results of an adaptive model are ______________.

A.

Priority and Propensity

B.

Priority and Evidence

C.

Propensity and Performance

D.

Propensity and Rank

Answer: C

Explanation:

QUESTION NO: 23

Predictive Analytics is a ______________ .

A.

real time predictive dashboard

B.

method of visualizing our data

C.

science concerned with finding repeatable patterns in data

D.

query, reporting and a search tool

Answer: C

Reference: https://pegasystems2.https.internapcdn.net/pegasystems2/marketing/C-762-StudentGuide.pdf (216)

QUESTION NO: 24

The mapping of the input fields of a third-party predictive model is done in the ______________ .

A.

Predictive Model decision component

B.

Predictive Model rule

C.

Predictive Analytics Director portal

D.

Customer class definition

Answer: B

Reference: https://community.pega.com/sites/default/files/help_v731/rule-/rule-decision-/rule-decision-predictivemodel/inputmapping.htm

QUESTION NO: 25

What format is used to express PMML?

A.

HTML

B.

SQL

C.

CSV

D.

XML

Answer: D

Reference: https://community1.pega.com/community/pega-support/question/creating-pmml-python-r-and-pega

QUESTION NO: 26

The performance of an Adaptive Model that has not collected any evidence is ____________.

A.

1.0

B.

0.0

C.

null

D.

0.5

Answer: D

Reference: https://pegasystems2.https.internapcdn.net/pegasystems2/marketing/C-762-
StudentGuide.pdf

QUESTION NO: 27

Which of the following is a good candidate for a predictor in a Scoring Model?

A.

Customer Date of Birth

B.

Mobile Phone Number

C.

Total International Minutes

D.

Customer Name

Answer: C

Explanation:

QUESTION NO: 28

What is Predictive Model Markup Language (PMML)?

A.

An Industry standard language used to represent predictive models

B.

Pega's own language used to represent predictive models

C.

A mathematics based language used to represent predictive models

D.

An XML-Based language used to represent predictive models

Answer: D

Reference: https://pegasystems2.https.internapcdn.net/pegasystems2/marketing/C-762-
StudentGuide.pdf (236)

QUESTION NO: 29

When configuring an Adaptive Model, the property type Integer is automatically translated to which
predictor type?

A.

Symbolic

B.

Numeric

C.

Alphanumeric

D.

Number

Answer: A

Reference: https://community1.pega.com/community/pega-academy/question/comparison-adaptive-
model-vs-predictive-model

QUESTION NO: 30

Pega Adaptive Models ______________.

A.

involve a significant human effort to develop

B.

require historical data

C.

learn about customer behavior in real time

D.

can only be used in inbound channels

Answer: C

Explanation:

QUESTION NO: 31

Which value is output by an Adaptive Model?

A.
Score

B.
Performance

C.
Behavior

D.
Lift

Answer: B

Reference: https://pegasystems2.https.internapcdn.net/pegasystems2/marketing/C-762-
StudentGuide.pdf (252)

QUESTION NO: 32

The Adaptive Model output that is automatically mapped to a strategy property is _______________.

A.
performance

B.
propensity

C.
evidence

D.
score

Answer: C

eference: https://pegasystems2.https.internapcdn.net/pegasystems2/marketing/C-762-udentGuide.pdf (251)

QUESTION NO: 33

When building a predictive model, the use of testing and validation samples _______________.

A.

increases the accuracy of models

B.

enables model validation in strategies

C.

is mandatory for segmentation

D.

validates the quality of input data

Answer: D

Reference: https://pegasystems2.https.internapcdn.net/pegasystems2/marketing/C-762-StudentGuide.pdf (223)

QUESTION NO: 34

The Adaptive Model instance is created when you ___________.

A.

execute the strategy containing the Adaptive Model component

B.

create an Adaptive Model rule

C.

configure an Adaptive Model decision component

D.

import an Adaptive Model definition rule

Answer: A

Explanation:

What is the most accurate description of proactive retention? Proactive Retention
________________.

A.

simplifies the process of retaining customers

B.

enables business to respond to customers when they contact a call center

C.

anticipates potential customer churn

D.

enables the business to reduce the number of credit risk customers

Answer: C

Reference: https://pegasystems2.https.internapcdn.net/pegasystems2/marketing/C-762-StudentGuide.pdf (206)

QUESTION NO: 36

Proactive retention is applicable when a customer is ____________.

A.

initiating contact to churn

B.

in a collections process

C.

likely to churn

D.

a high value customer

Answer: C

Reference: https://pegasystems2.https.internapcdn.net/pegasystems2/marketing/C-762-StudentGuide.pdf (208)

QUESTION NO: 37

The action a selling organization undertakes to reduce customer defections is also known as

_______________.

A.

marketing

B.

upselling

C.

cross-selling

D.

retention

Answer: D

Reference: https://pegasystems2.https.internapcdn.net/pegasystems2/marketing/C-762-StudentGuide.pdf (203)

QUESTION NO: 38

When building a predictive model, at what stage do you compare the performance of predictive models?

A.

Model Development stage

B.

Model Analysis stage

C.

Model Export stage

D.

Model Comparison stage

Answer: B

Explanation:

QUESTION NO: 39

When building a predictive model, the Data Analysis stage is where you _______________.

A.

create data samples

B.

select the input data

C.

group predictors

D.

determine the output field

Answer: C

Reference: https://pegasystems2.https.internapcdn.net/pegasystems2/marketing/C-762-StudentGuide.pdf (219)

QUESTION NO: 40

In an Adaptive Model rule, what is a valid predictor data type?

A.

Character

B.

Symbolic

C.

Boolean

D.

String

Answer: B

Explanation:

QUESTION NO: 41

In the delta view in Visual Business Director, what does the green colored shape indicate?

A.

The Reference data is valid.

B.

The Source data value is larger than the Reference data value.

C.

The Source data is valid.

D.

The Source data value is smaller than the Reference data value.

Answer: C

Reference: https://pegasystems2.https.internapcdn.net/pegasystems2/marketing/C-762-StudentGuide.pdf (124)

QUESTION NO: 42

In Pega Decision Management, individual customer behavior is captured by:

A.

Interaction history

B.

Visual Business Director

C.

Predictive models

D.

Decision strategies

Answer: C
Explanation:

QUESTION NO: 43

When configuring a Data Join component, the source of the join can be of which type?

A.

Component

B.

Strategy

C.

Proposition

D.

Property

Answer: A

Reference: https://pegasystems2.https.internapcdn.net/pegasystems2/marketing/C-762-
StudentGuide.pdf (200)

QUESTION NO: 44

The number of results returned by an Interaction History component can be narrowed down based on
_______________.

A.

the age of the customer

B.

a time period

C.

the customer lifetime value

D.

the total count of propositions in a given channel

Answer: B

Explanation:

QUESTION NO: 45

To extend a Customer data model with Product Holdings data, we need a _______________.

A.

Data Join

B.

Data Import

C.

D.

Join

Answer: A

Reference: https://pegasystems2.https.internapcdn.net/pegasystems2/marketing/C-762-
StudentGuide.pdf (200)

QUESTION NO: 46

In a decision strategy, the Switch component can ___________ .

A.

be used to test two strategies against each other

B.

make references to Switch decision components in other strategies

C.

be used to calculate the propensity

D.

be used to arbitrate between two decision logic paths

Answer: A

Reference: https://pegasystems2.https.internapcdn.net/pegasystems2/marketing/C-762-
StudentGuide.pdf (40)

QUESTION NO: 47

In a decision strategy, the Adaptive Model decision component belongs to the _______________ .

A.

Decision Analytics category

B.

Business Rules category

C.

Arbitration category

D.

Predictive Model category

Answer: A

Explanation:

QUESTION NO: 48

In Pega Customer Decision HubTM, the characteristics of a proposition are defined using
_______________.

A.
properties

B.
banners

C.
logos

D.
plain text

Answer: A

Explanation:

QUESTION NO: 49

The Prioritize component sorts offers in _______________.

A.
descending order only

B.
ascending or descending order

C.
random order

D.
ascending order only

swer: C

Explanation:

QUESTION NO: 50

If you would like to ensure that the strategy outputs at most one Proposition, the best component to achieve this is the _____________.

A.

It is not possible, unless you only have only one Proposition.

B.

Prioritize

C.

Switch

D.

Filter

Answer: C

Explanation:

QUESTION NO: 51

In a strategy defined in the "Retention" issue and the "X-Sell" group, you can import ____________.

A.

all propositions from the system

B.

propositions from "X-Sell" group

C.

propositions from all groups under "Retention" issue

D.

propositions from Sales issue

Answer: D

Explanation:

QUESTION NO: 52

In a decision strategy, which decision component both filters relevant offers and prioritizes these offers?

A.

Group By component

B.

Switch component

C.

Prioritize component

D.

Filter component

Answer: C

Explanation:

QUESTION NO: 53

When a customer is offered a proposition he has already accepted, this is because ___________.

A.

the strategy uses interaction history to exclude previously accepted offers

B.

the customer intent was captured incorrectly

C.

the propositions are filtered based on eligibility

D.

there is no filter for previously accepted offers in the strategy

Answer: D

Explanation:

QUESTION NO: 54

What does a dotted line from a "Group By" component to a "Filter" component mean?

A.

There is a one-to-one relationship between the "Group By" and the "Filter" components.

B.

To evaluate the "Group By" component, the "Filter" component is evaluated first.

C.

A property from the "Group By" is referenced by the "Filter" component.

D.

Information from the "Group By" is copied over to the "Filter" component.

Answer: A

Explanation:

QUESTION NO: 55

Aggregation components provide the ability to ____________.

A.

make calculations based upon a list of propositions

B.

set a text value to a strategy property

C.

filter propositions based on priority and relevance

D.

choose between propositions

Answer: A

Reference: https://pegasystems2.https.internapcdn.net/pegasystems2/marketing/C-762-
StudentGuide.pdf (p.177)

QUESTION NO: 56

The Prioritize component always outputs ____________.

A.

all eligible offers

B.

top 1 offer

C.

top 3 offer

D.

an arbitrary number of offers

Answer: A

Reference: https://pegasystems2.https.internapcdn.net/pegasystems2/marketing/C-762-StudentGuide.pdf (81)

QUESTION NO: 57

What is a proposition in Pega Customer Decision HubTM?

A.

Customer facing action

B.

Treatment

C.

Offers for sales, cross sell, or retention

D.

Service or retention offer

Answer: C

Explanation:

QUESTION NO: 58

To define the relationship between Customer and Product Usage, you must create the Product Usage property in the _____________.

A.

Product class

B.

C.

Customer class

D.

Product Usage class

Answer: D

Explanation:

QUESTION NO: 59

To use Product Holdings information in your strategy, which of the following components do you use?

A.

Data Import

B.

Decision Parameters

C.

Product Holdings

D.

Property Set

Answer: A

Reference: https://pegasystems2.https.internapcdn.net/pegasystems2/marketing/C-762-
StudentGuide.pdf (199)

QUESTION NO: 60

Which component belongs to the "Business Rules" decision component category?

A.

Contact policy

B.

Financial calculation

C.

Decision Table

D.

Decision data

Answer: C

Reference: https://pegasystems2.https.internapcdn.net/pegasystems2/marketing/C-762-
StudentGuide.pdf (35)

QUESTION NO: 61

Which function is available when configuring the Group By component?

A.

Multiply

B.

True if Some

C.

Divide

D.

Average

Answer: D

Reference: https://community.pega.com/sites/default/files/help_v719/rule-/rule-decision-/rule-
decision-strategy/components/aggregation.htm

QUESTION NO: 62

When executing a decision strategy, the blue dotted line in a decision strategy means

_______________.

A.

data is referenced by the component the arrow points to

B.

data is copied to the component the arrow points to

C.

data is copied to the component the arrow originates from

D.

data is referenced by the component the arrow originates from

Answer: A

Explanation:

QUESTION NO: 63

What is the key component of a Next-Best-Action strategy?

A.

Strategy

B.

Work flow

C.

Decision table

D.

Predictive model

Answer: D

Explanation:

QUESTION NO: 64

When implementing a Next-Best-Action project, which step is recommended to be taken first?

A.

Define Issue and Group hierarchy

B.

Define propositions

C.

Define business rules

D.

Define prioritization formula

nswer: A

Reference: https://pegasystems2.https.internapcdn.net/pegasystems2/marketing/C-762-StudentGuide.pdf

QUESTION NO: 65

When balancing the customer need with the business objective, a possible business objective is

______________.

A.
Social media

B.
Consistent communication

C.
Risk mitigation

D.
Timeliness

Answer: C

Reference: https://pegasystems2.https.internapcdn.net/pegasystems2/marketing/C-762-StudentGuide.pdf (14)

QUESTION NO: 66

When implementing Next-Best-Action, the Customer Lifetime Value Threshold is typically used to

______________.

A.
prioritize high value propositions

B.
prioritize customers

C.
determine if the customer is eligible

D.
calculate the customer's lifetime value

swer: C

Reference: https://pegasystems2.https.internapcdn.net/pegasystems2/marketing/C-762-
StudentGuide.pdf (51)

QUESTION NO: 67

What are the most important aspects taken into consideration when determining the Next-Best-Action?

A.

Product discounts and business profitability

B.

Network bandwidth and call duration

C.

Market trends and customer satisfaction

D.

Business objectives and customer needs

Answer: D

Explanation:

QUESTION NO: 68

Pega's ability to turn data into insight into action is known as:

A.

business rules

B.

adaptive analytics

C.

big data

D.

Next-Best-Action

Answer: D

Reference: https://pegasystems2.https.internapcdn.net/pegasystems2/marketing/C-762-
StudentGuide.pdf (15)

QUESTION NO: 69

Through analysis of customer lifecycles, Next-Best-Action _____________.

A.
anticipates retention issues

B.
provides future sales reports

C.
provides fulfillment services

D.
identifies global sales targets

Answer: A
Explanation:

QUESTION NO: 70

From two churn models with the similar performance, we choose the one with the ___________.

A.
highest churn rate

B.
highest number of predictors

C.
fewest number of predictors

D.
most evidence

Answer: A
Explanation:

QUESTION NO: 71

A Scoring Model allows you to differentiate between ____________.

A.

Accept, Reject, Maybe Later

B.

Good, Bad

C.

Good, Better, Best

D.

Good, Bad, Unknown

Answer: B

Reference: https://pegasystems2.https.internapcdn.net/pegasystems2/marketing/C-762-StudentGuide.pdf (220)

QUESTION NO: 72

The outcome of a scoring model indicates the likely ______________.

A.

write-off value of an arrears case

B.

claim value of a health insurance

C.

period in which a spare part has to be replaced

D.

response to an offer

Answer: D
Explanation:

QUESTION NO: 73

Adaptive model predictors are selected from the ____________.

communication channel

B.

similar propositions

C.

customer profile

D.

proposition profile

Answer: C

Explanation:

QUESTION NO: 74

To predict if a customer is likely to churn you use a model of type ______________.

A.

champion challenger

B.

decision tree

C.

switch

D.

decision table

Answer: D

Explanation:

QUESTION NO: 75

When building a predictive model, in which development step is the regression model created?

A.

Model Export

B.

C.

Model Analysis

D.

Model Development

Answer: D

Reference: https://pegasystems2.https.internapcdn.net/pegasystems2/marketing/C-762-StudentGuide.pdf (219)

QUESTION NO: 76

The result of a Predictive Model is stored in a property called _______________.

A.

pyPrediction

B.

pxResult

C.

pyOutcome

D.

pxSegment

Answer: D

Reference: https://pegasystems2.https.internapcdn.net/pegasystems2/marketing/C-762-StudentGuide.pdf (241)

QUESTION NO: 77

What happens when you increase the performance threshold setting of an adaptive model rule?

A.

The number of active predictors increases.

B.

The number of active predictors may decrease.

C.

The correlation threshold decreases.

D.

The performance of the model is increased.

Answer: B

Reference: https://pegasystems2.https.internapcdn.net/pegasystems2/marketing/C-762-StudentGuide.pdf (248)

QUESTION NO: 78

To create channel-specific Adaptive Model instances, you ______________.

A.

do nothing; Adaptive Model instances are always channel specific

B.

create channel specific Adaptive Model definition

C.

set channel information in the strategy

D.

set the channel option in the Adaptive Model component

Answer: D

Explanation:

QUESTION NO: 79

For an Adaptive Model to react quickly to changes in customer behavior, the ______________.

A.

performance threshold should be set to a low number

B.

model must always evaluate all customer responses

C.

strategy must include the calculation for smooth propensity

value of the memory setting should be set to a low number

Answer: A

Explanation:

QUESTION NO: 80

What is the key difference between a predictive model and a human expert?

A.

Predictive models always outperform human experts.

B.

Humans are better at dealing with structured data and identifying patterns.

C.

Predictive models are more capable of detecting patterns in historical data.

D.

Humans make successful predictions on a large amount of data.

Answer: B

Explanation:

QUESTION NO: 81

Which statement about predictive models is true?

A.

You need past experience to create a predictive model.

B.

They need unstructured big data.

C.

They are always associated with a proposition.

D.

They need to be specified in a data attribute.

Answer: A

Explanation:

QUESTION NO: 82

Which decision component allows you to use a third-party Credit Risk Model 80% of the time and a Pega Credit Risk Model 20%?

A.
Filter

B.
Champion Challenger

C.
Adaptive Model

D.
Switch

Answer: C
Explanation:

QUESTION NO: 83

Which decision component enables you to use a PMML model?

A.
Predictive Model

B.
PMML Model

C.
Third-party Model

D.
Adaptive Model

Answer: A
Reference: https://pegasystems2.https.internapcdn.net/pegasystems2/marketing/C-762-StudentGuide.pdf

QUESTION NO: 84

The point at which smooth propensity and actual propensity converge is when ___________.

A.

actual evidence is greater than starting evidence

B.

starting evidence is greater than actual evidence

C.

starting propensity is greater than actual propensity

D.

actual propensity is greater than starting propensity

Answer: A

Reference: https://pegasystems2.https.internapcdn.net/pegasystems2/marketing/C-762-StudentGuide.pdf (254)

QUESTION NO: 85

One of the purposes of the Interaction History decision component is to _____________.

A.

capture all interactions with the customer

B.

verify is a customer is eligible for an offer

C.

determine if a proposition has been offered before

D.

retrieve all proposition properties

Answer: C

Reference: https://pegasystems2.https.internapcdn.net/pegasystems2/marketing/C-762-StudentGuide.pdf (111)

QUESTION NO: 86

In a Set Property component, the Rank value is determined by ____________.

A.

the default value of the Rank

B.

the sequence in which it appears on the canvas

C.

the data transform

D.

the order in which the propositions are received

Answer: D

Reference: https://pegasystems2.https.internapcdn.net/pegasystems2/marketing/C-762-StudentGuide.pdf (176)

QUESTION NO: 87

To implement an eligibility criteria you use a ____________.

A.
Eligibility

B.
Segment

C.
Switch

D.
Proposition Filter

Answer: D

Explanation:

QUESTION NO: 88

reference a customer property in a strategy, you need to prefix the property name with the keyword _______________.

A.

No prefix. Use directly the property name.

B.

" "

C.

"Data."

D.

"Customer."

Answer: B

Reference: https://community.pega.com/sites/default/files/help_v731/designer-studio/expressionbuilder/ref_referprop_clipboard.htm

QUESTION NO: 89

Which category contains the Set Property component?

A.

Arbitration category

B.

Enrichment category

C.

Data Import category

D.

Business Rules category

Answer: B

Reference: https://pegasystems2.https.internapcdn.net/pegasystems2/marketing/C-762-StudentGuide.pdf (80)

QUESTION NO: 90

a decision strategy, to remove propositions based on the current month, you use a

____________.

A.

Calendar component

B.

Filter component

C.

date strategy property

D.

calendar strategy property

Answer: B

Explanation:

QUESTION NO: 91

What information has a 1-to-many relationship with a Customer?

A.

List of accounts owned

B.

Average monthly product usage

C.

Date of last visit to store

D.

Number of family members

Answer: A

Reference: https://pegasystems2.https.internapcdn.net/pegasystems2/marketing/C-762-StudentGuide.pdf (194)

QUESTION NO: 92

In Pega Decision Management, a banner on a website can represent ____________.

dimension

B.

strategy

C.

channel

D.

proposition

Answer: B

Explanation:

QUESTION NO: 93

In the Next-Best-Action strategy, a Switch component can be used to switch ______________.

A.

between two customers within the same household

B.

between two different service propositions

C.

between a high value and low value customer

D.

off interaction history

Answer: B

Explanation:

QUESTION NO: 94

In a Decisioning Strategy, which component is required to enable access to primary Customer properties?

A.

Set Property

B.

ne, properties are available

C.

Data Import

D.

Customer Import

Answer: A

Explanation:

QUESTION NO: 95

In a Decisioning Strategy, which component is required to enable access to Product Holding properties?

A.

Data Import

B.

None, properties are available

C.

Set Property

D.

Customer Import

Answer: A

Reference: https://pegasystems2.https.internapcdn.net/pegasystems2/marketing/C-762-StudentGuide.pdf (199)

QUESTION NO: 96

To access a property from an unconnected component, you use the ____________.

A.

customer-dot-property construct

B.

property value

C.

t-property value directly

D.

component name-dot-property construct

Answer: D

Reference: https://pegasystems2.https.internapcdn.net/pegasystems2/marketing/C-762-
StudentGuide.pdf (116)

QUESTION NO: 97

When a new component is added to the strategy canvas, its Rank value will be _______________.

A.

1

B.

One higher than the current highest Rank

C.

Not set

D.

0

Answer: A

Reference: https://pegasystems2.https.internapcdn.net/pegasystems2/marketing/C-762-
StudentGuide.pdf (176)

QUESTION NO: 98

To run a delta report in the Visual Business Director, a minimum of two ______________ are
required.

A.

data sources

B.

propositions

C.

input definitions

D.

strategies

Answer: D

Reference: https://pegasystems2.https.internapcdn.net/pegasystems2/marketing/C-762-StudentGuide.pdf (123)

QUESTION NO: 99

After launching a new product, the delta mode in Visual Business Director could show

_________________.

A.

the volume difference between the new product and the existing products

B.

the date when the new product was introduced

C.

the volume of the existing products

D.

a green shape for the product added

Answer: A

Reference: https://pegasystems2.https.internapcdn.net/pegasystems2/marketing/C-762-StudentGuide.pdf (131)

QUESTION NO: 100

Visual Business Director allows you to perform:

A.

What-if analysis

B.

Naive Bayesian analysis

C.

Predictive analysis

D.

Monte Carlo simulation

Answer: A

Reference: https://pegasystems2.https.internapcdn.net/pegasystems2/marketing/C-762-
StudentGuide.pdf